Bishop Mathews

Bishop James K. Mathews ... of the Methodist Church:

"All loyal Americans will have heard the tragic news of the assassination of President Kennedy with shock and amazement. One can scarcely realize that such an event could occur to our own Chief of State in his own country. It is almost impossible to conceive what maniacal incentive could have prompted so terrible a deed, one that will move the entire world to tears and to prayer.

"At the same time, we all must bear a measure of responsibility in view of our unwillingness to be the people ... was our religious heritage demands ... we be. We can only hope that ... from those responsible for this hideous crime will be brought to ... justice.

"This event of such magnitude and sorrow, must summon us all to our knees to pray for our President and our beloved country."

... that high yellow frame, was rolled ... into position.

Then at a few minutes after 6, U.S. Air Force 1, all white and blue, landed amid a deafening roar. The back door was flung open. But this time there was no familiar graceful figure fingering a button of his jacket, waiting to smile, waiting to wave.

Instead the light fell on the gleam of a bronze casket.

And around it, sharply outlined in the yellow frame of the cherry picker, stood the Old Guard of the dead President.

The light played on the bald head of David Powers, the President's pal, and his first political mentor, who 18 years ago towed him around the three decker flats of Everett and Charlestown, when the slender young Navy veteran was starting on the glory road.

On the other side of the bronze casket stood Lawrence F. O'Brien, since 1961 the President's congressional liaison man, but in the old days his chief organizer and vote counter.

With him was P. Kenneth O'Donnell who would have died for him, and who watched over hi mevery step of the long campaign trail that led to the White House.

At the foot of the coffin, white gloves sharp against her black suit, was Evelyn Lincoln, his secretary during the years in the White House.

The men picked up their unspeakable burden and placed it on top of the platform and it was lowered into the hearse.

Then in the frame stood his wife Jacqueline in a rose colored suit with black fac-

Casket

... of the Senate ... majority leader ... and his weeping ... whip Hum- ... Minnesota, who told ... President just be- ... for Texas had told ... feared for the life ... Belancourt of

Johnson, now bearing ... burden of the presidency, appeared pale and shaken. He boarded a helicopter with Sec. of Defense Robert F. McNamara and McGeorge Bundy, special assistant for National Security Affairs.

He immediately met in the White House with legislative leaders and staff at the Executive Office Building, an alley away from the White House.

The grieving Mrs. Kennedy departed from the airport with Atty. Gen. Robert Kennedy and together they rode in a Navy ambulance to Bethesda Naval Hospital where the President's body was to undergo an autopsy and remain overnight.

In the midst of the bereavement, her primary concern was for her children, John Jr. and Caroline who were still unaware of the tragedy early Friday night.

Mrs. Kennedy did not return to the White House but was not expected there, according to Andrew T. Hatcher, assistant press secretary.

Mrs. Kennedy remained overnight at the Naval Hospital in suburban Maryland, where she was placed under the care of her personal physician, Dr. John W. Walsh.

She is expected to return to the White House this morning. Atty. Gen. Kennedy also stayed with her. Officials said she was not under sedation.

Her two young children were taken from the White House shortly before the plane carrying their father's body landed at Andrews Air Force Base. Caroline, who will be six on Wednesday, and John Jr., who becomes three on Monday, were removed to an undisclosed place of seclusion.

Personal Triumph

President Kennedy was enjoying the fruits of political and personal satisfaction when the bullet from a high-

Children Knew

WASHINGTON (UPI)— Caroline Kennedy, who observes her sixth birthday anniversary next Wednesday, and her brother John Jr., who observes his third on Monday, were in the White House Friday when their father was assassinated.

Their mother, Mrs. Jacqueline Kennedy, it was assumed, reserved to herself the task of telling them what had happened.

Once before this year, there was a family tragedy to be told about. It was the death of their infant brother, Patrick Bovier Kennedy, last Aug. 9, two days after he had been born.

Children Her Thought

Her husband died as she waited outside the room where he lay inside, surgeons were ...

right and Jacqueline ... his left. Gov. John B. Connally of Texas was in the "jump seat" in front of the President, with Mrs. Conn ... to his left.

As the presidential ... moved into a triple-un ... pass, it slowed to 25 miles ... hour.

A sharp crack and the whine of a rifle shot was heard above the cheering. Then the sound of two more.

Charles Brehm, a spectator, viewed the result: "He was waving and the first shot hit him and then that awful look crossed his face."

In Jacqueline's Arms

The assassin's bullet tore a gaping hole in the back of his head and emerged through his neck. Impact of the slug sent him sprawling forward.

Mrs. Kennedy cried, "O, No!" She lifted his blood-smeared head into her arms.

Gov. Connally was hit by the other two bullets.

One bullet entered his chest and the other fractured his right wrist. Mrs. Connally put her arms around the governor.

As the driver, a Secret Service agent, accelerated the car out of rifle range and headed for the hospital, Mrs. Kennedy threw herself over the prostrate form of the President, as if to protect him.

Doctors later described Gov. Connally's condition as satisfactory although serious.

During the high-speed ride to Parkland Hospital, Mrs. Kennedy knelt on the floor of the car next to her husband. At the hospital, she helped lift him onto a stretcher, appearing stunned.

As the President was carried into the emergency room, Jacqueline walked behind the stretcher. Her clothing was spattered by blood.

He Loved Them

The children had looked forward to the new baby in the family, and it was their father who took them aside one day and told them there would be none.

Caroline and John Jr., if not too young, will have many memories to know how much their father loved them.

Jacqueline once said the President used to look at Caroline as though he couldn't believe she was true.

His affection for John Jr. has been especially apparent as the youngster grew old enough to dash in and out of the President's office, always curious, always eager to race off with his father.

Grieving then as now, she cancelled public appearances for the remainder of the year. But after a trip to Greece, she decided to accompany her husband to Texas for a two-day ...

Mr. Kennedy had flown to ... re Field outside Dallas from ... Air Force ... ly to the Texas ... where the President was to speak on his second day of politicking.

Crowds jammed the curbs. The Secret Service men ran alongside the car and watched from another car behind. Dallas motorcycle police formed a phalanx. But the assassin struck too swiftly, too treacherously for them.

Mrs. Kennedy had just leaned over to her husband and said, "You can't say Dallas wasn't friendly to you," when three shots rang out.

Charles Brehm, 38, of Dallas was standing in the crowd at curbside about 15 feet away as the President's car approached.

"He was waving and then that awful look crossed his face," Brehm said.

Kennedy fell over sideways on his face toward the seat. Doctors said later that one shot apparently had torn through both the back of his head and his throat. Mrs. Kennedy screamed.

Gov. Connally fell face forward to the floor of the car

By MERRIMAN SMITH

WASHINGTON (UPI) —The soul of John Fitzgerald Kennedy was commended unto God today at a simple Roman Catholic funeral Mass attended by world leaders.

Last rites for the assassinated President were conducted at St. Matthew's Cathedral by Richard Cardinal Cushing of Boston, lifelong friend and pastor who officiated at Mr. Kennedy's marriage ceremony and baptized his children.

Secret Service ... Greet at the wheel ... automobile whirled the ca ... the Parkland Hos ... the President's ... physician, Rear ... George Burkley, in a car ...

Mrs. Kennedy, her pink wool suit splattered blood, cradled her hus head and stroked his and, at the hospital, she to him and helped lift a stretcher.

Police said Oswald, and sullen, denied hav thing to do with the as tion, but admitted he in the building from w fatal shots were fi would not account whereabouts at the ti assassination, police

Oswald was seized in a theater in the district of Dallas less miles from the sce assassination.

A policeman, J. 38, was shot down about five blocks Texas Theater. T cashier, Mrs. Juli reported to police cious man had theater. Four po cluding Tippitt, him.

After shooting cording to police,

Mr. Ken ... draped caske ... to the cathe ... White Hous ... away, by the ... drawn caisso ... the remains ... to! where ... 240,000 per ... the bier.

Mrs. Ja ... nedy, who ... hand's sid ... bullet on ... day, folle ... hind the

At he

A Syn

By HELEN THOMAS

WASHINGTON (UPI) —Mrs. Jacqueline Kennedy passed her final ordeal today.

The widow of the nation's 35th President bore heroically the burden of her grief, but found it di ... to surrender his ...

She ... separate ... Twice ... the Cap ... flag-sh

Mrs. ... of kir ... forme ... the bu ... who ... and

Never Any Hope

Inside, she grasped the hands ... who was to suc-

KENNEDY

ASSASSINATED!

The World Mourns

A Reporter's Story

Wilborn Hampton

CANDLEWICK PRESS
CAMBRIDGE, MASSACHUSETTS

For Jack Fallon, who gave me a chance

Additional photo captions:

Pg. 1   Simulation of Oswald's view of the President's limo taken by the Warren Commission as part of the assassination investigation

Pg. 2   President Kennedy being greeted by an enthusiastic crowd in Fort Worth on November 22, 1963, before leaving for Dallas

Pg. 91 The eternal flame in front of John Fitzgerald Kennedy's grave at Arlington National Cemetery

First edition 1997

Library of Congress Cataloging-in-Publication Data

Hampton, Wilborn.
Kennedy assassinated! : the world mourns : a reporter's story / Wilborn Hampton.
Includes bibliographical references and index.
ISBN 1-56402-811-9
1. Kennedy, John F. (John Fitzgerald), 1917–1963—
Assassination—Juvenile literature. I. Title.
E842.9.H265   1997
364.1'524'097309046—dc20   96–25801

4 6 8 10 9 7 5 3

Printed in Hong Kong / China

This book was typeset in Berling.
Design and photo research by Ann Stott

Candlewick Press
2067 Massachusetts Avenue
Cambridge, Massachusetts 02140

John Fitzgerald Kennedy, 1917–1963, 35th President of the United States

Introduction

For each generation there are one or two moments in time that become fixed in memory. Either because the event that occurred then was so devastating or because it marked a turning point in the course of history, that moment becomes both a universal point of reference and an intimately personal memory. Years later, the very mention of it can bring to mind with minute precision exactly what you were doing when you heard the news, whom you were with, what you said or felt, whether you wept.

For one generation of Americans, my parents' generation, such a moment was December 7, 1941, the date President Franklin Delano Roosevelt said would live in infamy, the day Japanese warplanes bombed Pearl Harbor and brought the United States into World War II. A generation before that, for Europeans, such a date might have been June 28, 1914, the day the Archduke Franz Ferdinand was assassinated in Sarajevo in what became known as the first shot of World War I.

And for anyone old enough to remember in the present generation of parents and grandparents, such a day and hour was November 22, 1963, at 12:34 P.M., central standard time.

A Harvard student weeps upon hearing the news of Kennedy's assassination.

President and Mrs. Kennedy riding in the open bubbletop limousine through Dallas.

Chapter 1

Certainly I will never forget where I was that day. I was standing by the news desk in the Dallas office of United Press International, mostly trying to stay out of the way.

Bill Hampton in 1963

I had been working at U.P.I. for only two months. News agencies like U.P.I. and the Associated Press, U.P.I.'s chief rival, provide news stories to newspapers and television and radio stations. It was my first job after finishing the University of Texas in Austin that summer, and I was still learning the ropes.

It had been very hectic in the office for the previous two days. President John F. Kennedy was making a highly publicized trip to Texas, going to five cities and making a major speech in Dallas. The Presidential visit was what was called in those days a fence-mending trip. The Texas governor, John B. Connally, and the state's senior senator, Ralph Yarborough, were involved in a political feud that even Kennedy's vice president, Lyndon B. Johnson, who was also from Texas, couldn't patch up. So Kennedy himself was coming to the state to try to reconcile them. Connally, Yarborough, and Johnson were all traveling with the President in a public display of unity.

*Texas Governor
John B. Connally*

*Texas Senator Ralph
Yarborough*

*Vice President
Lyndon B. Johnson*

Everybody in the Dallas office had been busy on the story. Everybody, that is, except me. Since I was the most inexperienced reporter on the staff, I did not have a lot to do with covering Kennedy's trip. As a result, I had felt like a fifth wheel around the office since the President had arrived in Texas.

The only part I had played so far in covering the President's visit was to take some dictation over the telephone the previous day from Merriman Smith, who was U.P.I.'s chief White House reporter. But that was about to change in the next couple of minutes. In fact, my whole life was about to change.

Merriman Smith was known to everyone by his nickname, Smitty, and he had been covering Presidents since Roosevelt. Since he was the senior White House reporter, Smitty always traveled with the President and always rode in the press car in Presidential motorcades, right next to the car phone, which was still a rare enough item to be considered modern technology. After taking the dictation from him, I gave Smitty's notes to Preston McGraw, who was known as Mac, to turn into a news story.

Everyone else had worked late the previous night. But when I had asked Jack Fallon, the U.P.I. division news manager, if he wanted me to stay and help out too, he told me no, I could go on home. It was a disappointment to me.

So, there I was, standing by the news desk, while there was a lull in the Dallas office. President Kennedy had arrived at Love Field, the Dallas airport, on a five-minute flight from Fort Worth, and he was at that moment driving through downtown

Dallas in a motorcade on his way to the Trade Mart, where he was to make his speech. Governor Connally was riding with him.

There had been a flurry of activity in the office with the President's takeoff from Fort Worth, where he had spent the previous night, and his arrival in Dallas. Although Dallas was considered hostile political territory to Kennedy, a large crowd turned out to greet him at Love Field. Jackie Kennedy was given a bouquet of roses and both the President and the First Lady went over to shake hands with some of the people at the airport.

And all along the motorcade route through downtown Dallas,

President and Mrs. Kennedy accompanied by Governor Connally being welcomed by Dallas city officials

The Kennedys and Governor Connally departing Love Field

thousands of people lined the sidewalks along Main Street to see the President as he drove by. Smitty had even called in from the telephone in the press car to dictate a paragraph to Jack Fallon about how surprisingly large the crowds were.

But the office was quiet now, everyone relaxing for a few minutes until the President arrived at the Trade Mart, and the frenzy of covering an American President would resume.

So I was alone as I stood by the news desk that day. I was wondering whether I should offer to get sandwiches for the rest of the office from the diner across the street, and whether I would get to stay and help out that night when the President flew on to Austin, the last stop on his trip.

Suddenly the telephone rang. I picked up the receiver and answered, "U.P.I."

I immediately recognized Smitty's voice from the day before. But this time Smitty was shouting.

"Bulletin precede!" Smitty yelled. "Three shots were fired at the motorcade!"

President Kennedy is hit by a bullet fired from the Texas School Book Depository, located off to the right.

In a sequence of photos taken from an 8 mm home movie, Secret Service agent Clinton J. Hill is shown leaping onto the rear of the Presidential limousine while Mrs. Kennedy reaches across the trunk to him. The agent pushes Mrs. Kennedy back into the car and protects her with his own body.

Chapter 2

There are some things in life for which there simply is no preparation. Certainly there was never anything in any of the journalism courses that I took in college or in my orientation at U.P.I. that covered what to do in case you received such a telephone call.

Many years have passed since that day, but I can still hear Smitty's voice on the other end of the line, syllable by syllable, his very tone screaming the urgency of the message, conveying that the news he had was a matter of life and death. And not just any life, not just any death, but that of the President of the United States.

Despite what I did next, I understood Smitty perfectly. His words were so terrifying that I nearly dropped the phone. I clutched it tightly in my hand and almost screwed the receiver in my ear. I turned and looked around the office. Preston McGraw was sitting across the newsroom reading a paper. Don Smith and Phil Newman, two other journalists in the Dallas office, were at the coffee machine. Jim Tolbert, the teletype operator, was sitting at the A-wire, the main news wire, typing a story into tape. Jack Fallon was standing at a telex machine, typing out a message to the U.P.I. office in Austin.

My survey of the office took maybe five seconds, which was probably about four seconds too long. I knew I had to act.

Cradling the phone on my shoulder, I grabbed what we called a book—four sheets of paper separated by carbons— from the news desk and nervously rolled it into a typewriter. I had to say something to Smitty, who was still shouting on the other end of the line. Two things prompted what I finally said. I wanted to confirm what I had heard. And I wanted to buy a little time. But time is the one thing I didn't have.

"What?" I shouted back. "I can't hear you."

"Three shots were fired at the motorcade!" Smitty screamed even louder. "Make it Bulletin precede!"

I started to type.

```
BULLETIN PRECEDE
DALLAS, NOV. 22 (UPI)--THREE SHOTS WERE
FIRED TODAY AT PRESIDENT KENNEDY'S
MOTORCADE IN DOWNTOWN DALLAS.
```

"I can't hear you," I said again, pronouncing each word slowly, as though I were speaking to a deaf man.

Smitty screamed the same information, and this time added the instructions "Repeat my Bulletin back to me!"

Smitty was afraid that his scoop was slipping away from him because of a bad phone connection between the press car and the U.P.I. office, or because some new kid in the office didn't know what he was doing.

Merriman
"Smitty" Smith

I yanked the book out of the typewriter, ripped off the top copy, and thrust it in front of Jim Tolbert. Jim read the two lines I had given him and reached down and tore off the tape of the story he had been typing from the machine. Without saying another word, he began punching the Bulletin into tape.

I put down the phone and stepped quickly over to Jack Fallon, who was still on the telex to Austin.

"Jack," I said. "Smitty's on the phone."

"What does he want?" Jack snapped, still hunched over the telex machine.

Jack Fallon

"He says three shots were fired at the motorcade," I said.

"What!" Jack straightened up. "Where is he?"

I held the phone out to Jack who grabbed it and leaped to a typewriter.

"I wrote this," I said and handed him a copy of the Bulletin.

Jack took a quick look at it, nodded his head and barked two words to Jim Tolbert: "Send it!"

A story about a murder trial in Minneapolis was moving on the A-wire. Jim pressed the little lever that would stop the story in progress, cut it off in midsentence. Like an emergency cord on a train, the "break" lever was rarely used. It was reserved strictly for Bulletins, for news that was so important it could not wait for even a minute. Jim hit the send button, then rang five bells on the machine to signify it was a Bulletin.

It was 12:34 P.M., central standard time.

A cameraman stands at the left and spectators crouch on the ground moments after a sniper's bullets are fired at the motorcade.

Chapter 3

Suddenly, the office sprang into action like a bomb had gone off. If Don, Mac, Phil, and the others had not heard what I had said to Jack, they heard Jack shout his order to Jim and the five bells on the teletype machine that always preceded and followed a Bulletin.

Jack leaped to a typewriter and rolled in a book. Smitty was apparently still demanding someone to read his Bulletin back to him, because Jack repeated those dozen words into the phone in a voice that sounded like a drill sergeant giving orders.

Phil and Mac grabbed telephones and started calling the local radio stations to see if their mobile news units had any more information on the shots. Don raced around behind Jack so he could read the adds to the story as they came out of his typewriter and relay them to Jim at the teletype machine. Judd Dixon, the broadcast editor, was typing out the Bulletin on the radio wire and Jerry McNeill, the U.P.I. picture manager, began calling the local papers to see if their photographers had any pictures U.P.I. could buy. Everybody in the office was racing around in furious activity. Everybody, that is, except me.

After handing the phone to Jack, I sort of moved into the background. In fact, I was feeling miserable. I felt I had botched the phone call. I had taken too long to get the Bulletin written and handed to Jim. I should have given the phone to Jack immediately and not wasted all that time telling Smitty I couldn't hear him. The whole thing had taken maybe a minute, and it was the longest minute of my life.

Jack was carrying on a loud phone conversation with Smitty, both of them shouting as though they were trying to talk across a noisy, crowded room. Jack was asking Smitty whether anyone had been hit by the shots and what Smitty could see from the press car, which was about five cars behind the President's open convertible. For reasons I learned only later, it was almost impossible for Smitty to see anything that was going on. The motorcade sped up, heading in the direction of the Trade Mart. Meanwhile, after moving that first Bulletin, the A-wire was ominously silent.

Jack knew this. But he also knew there was only one question to which editors in newsrooms all over the world wanted the answer: Had President Kennedy been hit by the shots?

The five bells that had rung on the teletype machines with the Bulletin had alerted editors that a major story was breaking. The questions the Bulletin raised remained unanswered as seconds ticked into minutes and no add to the story appeared.

What I didn't know, and no one in the office did at that point, was that despite the slight delay caused by my nervousness and inexperience, U.P.I. was still all alone with the

A U.P.I. teletype machine

story. The reason for that was that Smitty was holding on to the phone in the press car.

When the shots were fired, Smitty had grabbed the car phone and called the Dallas office. After he reported the Bulletin, the Associated Press reporter, Jack Bell, who was also in the press car, began demanding the phone so he could call the Dallas A.P. office. But Smitty pretended it was a bad connection and that was one reason he kept shouting "repeat my Bulletin back to me" long after Fallon assured him it was already on the wire. The longer Smitty could hold on to the phone in the press car and keep it away from Jack Bell, the longer he had a scoop on possibly the biggest story of his career.

As Smitty began to order the driver of the press car to pass the other cars in the motorcade, so he could get closer to the President's limousine, Jack Bell began trying to pull the phone out of Smitty's hands. Smitty dropped to the floor of the car. As the press car sped up, Jack Bell reached over and tried to wrestle the phone away from Smitty. Smitty curled up in a fetal position, protecting the phone while Jack Bell began to grab at it. This fight was the reason Smitty could not see much of what was going on around him.

Meanwhile, neither Mac nor Phil were having any luck finding out more information. The local radio stations had heard the first news of the shots from U.P.I. and they knew nothing more. If Smitty, who was only a few cars away, couldn't find out what had happened, it was unlikely that local radio news units would have any more information. Even the press office at the police department knew only what had been on the radio.

Jack knew he had to get an add on the wire. Smitty told Jack that the motorcade was proceeding along its planned route toward the Trade Mart. Jack started writing.

```
URGENT
1ST ADD SHOTS
NO CASUALTIES WERE REPORTED.
THE INCIDENT OCCURRED NEAR THE
COUNTY SHERIFF'S OFFICE ON
MAIN STREET, JUST EAST OF AN
UNDERPASS LEADING TOWARD
THE TRADE MART WHERE THE
PRESIDENT WAS . . .
```

Sometimes, inspiration can strike right out of the blue. Even today, I have no clue how the idea came to me. But suddenly I knew the one person who would know what was happening. I might not get put through to that person, but I knew whom to call.

I grabbed one of the telephones and dialed the main number of the Dallas Police Department. A woman answered and I summoned all the authority I could muster into my voice.

"Give me Dispatch!"

Although the Secret Service is always responsible for the President's security, they work with local police departments when the President travels, for crowd and traffic control. The police also provide motorcycle escorts for motorcades. The police escort riding alongside the President's car would have reported in by radio phone to the dispatch office.

I was surprised when a man actually came on the line and said, "Dispatch."

"Bill Hampton of U.P.I. What can you tell me about the shots fired at the President's motorcade?" I asked, again trying to sound authoritative.

"The President has been hit," he said, matter-of-factly. "They are taking him to Parkland Hospital."

"How serious is it?"

"I don't know. I just got off the phone with a motorcycle officer right next to the limousine. He said there was blood in the back of the car. Governor Connally was also wounded. They are on their way to Parkland."

I should have had about a hundred questions. I was talking

to the one man who would know firsthand from a policeman right next to the President's car what was happening. But for maybe five seconds I couldn't think of anything to ask him. He had just told me the President of the United States had been shot, that there was blood in the back seat of the car and they were taking the President to the hospital. I was speechless.

"We really don't know any more," the dispatcher said. "I've got to clear this line."

"Okay," I replied. "Thanks."

"Sure thing," he said and disconnected the call.

Even before I hung up the receiver I called down the news desk to Jack Fallon.

"Jack, the police say Kennedy's been hit!"

Jack, who was still on the phone to Smitty, didn't look up. He continued to type, and clearly had not heard what I said. But Don Smith had heard me, and because he was relaying the copy to Jim Tolbert at the teletype machine, he knew that Smitty was reporting that no one was apparently injured. Don spoke up.

"Jack!" he shouted in Fallon's ear. "Listen to Bill."

Jack looked up with annoyance. "What is it?"

"The police say Kennedy's been hit and they're taking him to Parkland Hospital."

"What police?" Jack half rose out of his chair.

"The dispatcher. He had just talked to a motorcycle cop next to the motorcade. He said there was blood in the back of the car and Kennedy and Connally were both hit and they're going to Parkland."

JFK's limousine speeds toward Parkland Hospital moments after the shooting.
The President's foot is visible over the rear wheel.

"Smitty says they're on the motorcade route," Jack said, challenging me. "They're going toward the Trade Mart."

Although he had lived in Dallas a few years, Jack was from New York City and probably never had occasion to know where Parkland Hospital was. Smitty likely had never been to Dallas in his life. But I was from Dallas and knew the city well.

"It's the same way," I said.

"What's the same way?" Jack asked, his jaw clenched, knowing he had a major decision coming up in about ten seconds.

"Parkland," I said. "It's the same way as the Trade Mart. It's a couple of exits farther on the freeway."

Jack didn't say anything, but hurled a question back into the phone to Smitty.

"Smitty, what can you see from the car right now?"

"Smitty says they've passed the Trade Mart," Jack announced to no one in particular.

He looked up at me for maybe two seconds, as though making a decision, then ordered, "Go to Parkland."

Although he didn't give me specific instructions what to do when I got there, I did not wait around to ask if there were any. I knew I had just been assigned to help cover the story and I was out the door before he could change his mind.

As Don Smith told me later, I was gone only a couple of minutes when Smitty called in from the hospital. A Secret Service agent had told Smitty the President was badly wounded and likely wouldn't make it. Jack made a momentous decision. He stopped writing the new Bulletin in his typewriter, stood, and shouted, "Flash!"

Without looking around, Jim hit the break lever on the teletype, typed the word FLASH, and waited for Jack to continue.

"Flash!" Jack repeated, and Jim typed it a second time.

A U.P.I. teletype printer

```
FLASH
KENNEDY SERICUSLY WOUNDED
PERHAPS FATALLY BY ASSASSINS BULLET
```

It was 12:39 P.M., central standard time, five minutes after the first Bulletin moved, seven minutes after I had answered the telephone, nine minutes after a loner and a drifter named Lee Harvey Oswald had squeezed the trigger of the 6.5 millimeter Mannlicher-Carcano Italian carbine he had bought from a mail-order house in Chicago.

```
UPI 9N
BULLETIN
  1ST LEAD SHOOTING
    DALLAS, NOV. 22 (UPI)--PRESIDENT KENNEDY AND GOV. JOHN B. CONNALLY
OF TEXAS WERE CUTDOWN BY AN ASSASSIN'S BULLETS AS THEY TOURED
DOWNTOWN DALLAS IN AN OPEN AUTOMOBILE TODAY.
                             MOREJT1241PCS




UPI.A1ON DA
            1ST ADD 1ST LEAD SHOOTING DALLAS (9N DALLAS XX TODAY.
    THE PRESIDENT, HIS LIMP BODY CRADLED IN THE ARMS OF HIS WIFE, WAS
RUSHED TO PARKLAND HOSPITAL.  THE GOVERNOR ALSO WAS TAKEN TO PARKLAND.
    CLINT HILL, A SECRET SERVICE AGENT ASSIGNED TO MRS. KENNEDY, SAID
"HE'S DEAD," AS THE PRESIDENT WAS LIFTED FROM THE REAR OF A WHITE HOUSE
TOURING CAR, THE FAMOUS "BUBBLETOP" FROM WASHINGTON.  HE WAS RUSHED
TO AN EMERGENCY ROOM IN THE HOSPITAL.
    OTHER WHITE HOUSE OFFICIALS WERE IN DOUBT AS THE CORRIDORS OF THE
HOSPITAL ERUPTED IN PANDEMONIUM.
    THE INCIDENT OCCURRED JUST EAST OF THE TRIPLE UNDERPASS FACING A
PARK IN DOWNTOWN DALLAS.
    REPORTERS ABOUT FIVE CAR LENGTHS BEHIND THE CHIEF EXECUTIVE
HEAR
MORE 144PES




UPI A11N DA
            2ND ADD 1ST LEAD SHOOTING (9N DALLAS) XXX DALLAS.
    REPORTERS ABOUT FIVE CAR LENGTHS BEHIND THE CHIEF EXECUTIVE
HEARD WHAT WOUNDED LIKE THREE BURST OF GUNFIRE.
    SECRET SERVICE AGENTS IN A FOLLOW-UP CAR QUICKLY UNLIMBERED THEIR
AUTOMATIC RIFLES.
    THE BUBBLE TOP OF THE PRESIDENT'S CAR WAS DOWN.
    THEY DREW THEIR PISTOLS, BUT THE DAMAGE WAS DONE.
    THE PRESIDENT WAS SLUMPED OVER IN THE BACKSEAT OF THE CAR FACE
DOWN.  CONNALLY LAY ON THE FLOOR OF THE REAR SEAT.
    IT WAS IMPOSSIBLE TO TELL AT
MORE 145PES




UPI A12N DA

    IT WAS IMPOSSIBLE TO TELL AT ONCE WHERE KENNEDY WAS HIT, BUT BULLET
WOUNDS IN CONNALLY'S CHEST WERE PLAINLY VISIBLE, INDICATING THE GUNFIRE
MIGHT POSSIBLY HAVE COME FROM AN AUTOMATIC WEAPON.
    THERE WERE THREE LOUD BURSTS.
    DALLAS MOTORCYCLE OFFICERS ESCORTING THE PRESIDENT QUICKLY LEAPED
FROM THEIR BIKES AND RACED UP A GRASSY HILL.

    MORE 146PES




UPIA13N DA
```

A bouquet of roses presented to Lady Bird Johnson upon her arrival in Dallas
lying on the seat of the Vice President's limousine after its arrival at Parkland Hospital

The U.P.I. office at that time was on McKinney Avenue, north of the main downtown area of Dallas, and although no such records were likely kept, I doubt anyone has made the distance from McKinney to Parkland Hospital faster than I did that day.

As soon as Jack told me to go to Parkland, I raced across the newsroom, ran down the steps from the second floor office three at a time, jumped in my '56 Chevy, made a U-turn in the middle of the street, and sped toward the hospital.

Weaving in and out of traffic, honking my horn and passing cars, I reached Harry Hines Boulevard, the broad, busy thoroughfare that runs in front of the hospital, only to find it jammed with bumper-to-bumper traffic.

Hundreds of people who had heard the news on their radio had gotten in their car and already made their way to the hospital, driving in slow procession past the building, the way motorists inch past a car wreck, craning their neck to see nothing, but to be able to tell friends, family, and children not yet born that they had been there that day and had seen it all.

I knew I would never find a parking place around the hospital, so I drove across two lanes of traffic and up on the median strip that divided the boulevard. I turned off the ignition and left my car there. Maybe it would be there when I returned. Maybe not. But what I had to do was more important.

Although I knew that I was being sent simply as a reinforcement to help Smitty cover the story, all the way to the hospital one thought kept recurring in my mind: There was really only one vital fact to find out and that was whether the President of the United States was alive or dead.

I jogged across the huge lawn in front of the hospital to the rear, where I knew the emergency entrance was located.

There were dozens of people milling around, many of them nurses and hospital personnel in white coats. Several men in business suits carried guns; others had notebooks and pens. Some people stood in little groups of twos or threes, talking in low voices if not actual whispers. Others just stood alone. An ambulance was parked in one of the emergency bays. The President's limousine was nearby, one door still open, a bouquet of roses strewn on the back seat.

I knew the first thing I should do was to find Smitty. The problem was that although I had spoken to him twice on the phone, I had no idea what he looked like.

My plan was to get inside the emergency area and ask for him there. I headed toward the entrance under a sign that said Ambulances Only. Secret Service agents with submachine guns

Secret Service agents and reporters waiting for word on the President's condition at the emergency entrance at Parkland Hospital

stood blocking the way. No one was being allowed in or out.

Then I noticed that several of the men outside had little nametags on their suits, identification badges for members of the White House press corps. I went up to a man wearing one and asked him if he knew Merriman Smith.

The man gave me a withering look and said curtly, "I haven't seen him."

"I'm from the Dallas U.P.I. office," I explained. "If you could just point him out to me."

"I said I haven't seen him," the man snapped and turned away as if to dismiss me.

I looked more closely at his nametag. It said "Jack Bell, Associated Press."

For the next few minutes, I just stood outside the emergency entrance making a few notes, but feeling rather helpless. Then, there was a commotion and a Roman Catholic priest came out. He was immediately surrounded by reporters firing questions at him.

A Roman Catholic priest, leaving Parkland Hospital

I elbowed my way close to the center of the circle. There was such pushing and shoving it was hard to hear what was said. The priest gave his name, but I could not hear it. The other reporters were asking all sorts of questions: Were doctors operating on Kennedy? Where was he hit? How bad were his wounds? Was he conscious? The priest said he had given Kennedy the last rites of the Roman Catholic Church. And then he said what everyone had most feared. He said he believed the President was already dead.

I knew I should get the priest's name, but as I turned to ask the man next to me, I saw several reporters breaking away from the circle and trotting toward the corner of the building.

Barred from entering the hospital through the emergency room by the Secret Service agents, reporters were heading around the building toward the main entrance to look for phones. I would have to find Smitty later. I had to report what the priest said without any delay. I had to find a telephone. I ran after the other reporters.

For the first time that day my youth was an asset. It was a good quarter of a mile around the huge hospital from the emergency entrance to the main doors. There would be some pay phones in the lobby, and the reporters who got there first would get them. Most of the reporters were huffing and puffing as they jogged toward the front of the hospital. I ran for my life and passed them like they were standing still. I was all alone by the time I burst through the front doors of Parkland Hospital.

I spotted a pay phone in a little booth off to the right and dodged into it, feeling like Clark Kent about to change into Superman. I dialed the U.P.I. office and Don Smith answered.

"Don, a priest just came out of the emergency room and said Kennedy was dead," I sputtered, out of breath. "I didn't get his name," I added, a bit more subdued.

"Yeah, okay," Don said, then spoke away from the phone across the newsroom. Don seemed to be taking this news with considerably less urgency than I thought he should.

"Don," I persisted, "this priest said Kennedy was dead. He said he gave him last rites. He was in the emergency room."

There was a brief pause on the other end of the line. Don seemed to be listening to someone, probably Jack, talking to him in the newsroom.

"Listen, Bill, we already have what the priest said. Smitty phoned it in a few minutes ago. Smitty managed to get into the emergency area and found a phone there. We're not going with the priest. We're reporting what he said, but he's not official. He could be wrong. We have to get it from the White House or the hospital."

Don had another conversation with someone in the office, then came back on the line.

"Jack says you should try to find Smitty. Is there some way for you to get down to the emergency area?"

"I don't know," I replied. "I can try. I'm up in the main lobby now. The back entrance is blocked off, but maybe I can get down there from here."

"Try to hook up with Smitty," Don said. "By the way, Mac is on his way to the hospital, too. So you might look for him."

Just as I was about to hang up the receiver and charge off looking for Smitty, I glanced up at the dial wheel on the telephone, which all pay phones had in those days before push-button phones. It had a little card in the center with the number of the pay phone written in it. For the second time that day I had an inspiration.

"Don!" I shouted into the receiver.

"What?"

"Listen, phones are going to be impossible around here. I'm at a pay phone in the lobby. Let me give you the number, then you call me here from the office and we can tie up this phone."

In those days, the person who placed a phone call had to hang up to break the connection. If Don called me from the office, the line would remain tied up until Don hung up. Anyone who picked up that telephone in the lobby of Parkland Hospital would find himself talking to the Dallas office of U.P.I. and no amount of dimes would connect him to anyone else.

I read Don the phone number and hung up. About ten seconds later he called back. On his end, Don Smith tucked the receiver between his left ear and shoulder and braced himself for a long afternoon of waiting. I went off in search of Smitty or Mac.

<u>AUTOPSY</u>

NMS # A ___ ___ DATE _ _2-6_ HR. STARTED _____ HR. COMPLETED _____

NAME: _____ RANK/RATE _____

DATE/HOUR EXPIRED: _____ WARD _____ DIAGNOSIS _____

PHYSICAL DESCRIPTION: RACE: _____ Obtain following on babies only:
                                    Color
Height_____in. Weight_____lb. Hair_____   Crown-rump _____ in.
                                            Crown-heel _____ in.
Color eyes_____ Pupil Rt_____mm, Lt._____mm Circumference:
                                            Head_____in. Chest_____in.
WEIGHTS: (Grams, unless otherwise specified) Abd._____in.

LUNG, RT. __320   KIDNEY, RT. _135_   ADRENALS, RT. _____

LUNG, LT. __290   KIDNEY, LT. _140_   ADRENALS, LT. _____

BRAIN _____   LIVER _150_   PANCREAS _____

SPLEEN _90_   HEART _50_   THYROID _____

THYMUS _____ TESTIS _____   OVARY _____

HEART MEASUREMENTS: A _7.5_ cm. P _9_ cm. T _12_ cm. M _10_ cm.

              LVM _1.5_ cm.   RVM _.4_ cm.

NOTES:

Pathologist _____

As reporters rushed around the hospital looking for telephones, the real life and death drama of that day had already been played out downstairs in Emergency Room One. Although no reporters were in that room, what happened was pieced together in the hours, days, and weeks afterward from interviews with people who had been there.

When the call came in that President Kennedy had been shot and was on his way in, the loudspeaker crackled throughout the hospital to summon Dr. Thomas Shires, the chief surgeon at Parkland.

"Dr. Shires! STAT!" the announcement kept repeating. But Dr. Shires was out of town.

Dr. Malcolm Perry, who was Dr. Shires's assistant, was having lunch in the hospital cafeteria when he heard the call. Known as Mac to his friends, Dr. Perry was one of the hospital's brightest surgeons. He went straight to the emergency area and found the President was already on a surgical table.

As Dr. Perry strode into the room, he took off his plaid sports coat and dropped it to the floor. A nurse helped him

Dr. Malcolm Perry

Dr. Kemp Clark

into a pair of surgical gloves. He looked at the man on the table. The President had been stripped to the waist and his shoes had been removed. Another surgeon, Dr. Charles Carrico, was already at work and had put a breathing tube down the President's mouth.

Dr. Perry stepped up and took charge.

Outside in the corridor, people were rushing around. One Secret Service man waved a gun, giving orders that everyone ignored. Down the hall, in Emergency Room Two, other surgeons were working on Governor Connally.

There were now more than a dozen people crowded into Emergency Room One. Among them was Jacqueline Kennedy. Her skirt was spattered with blood and she looked dazed. She was not crying, but was staring straight ahead at her husband on the operating table. Dr. Kemp Clark, a neurosurgeon at the hospital, stepped over to Mrs. Kennedy and asked whether she might prefer to wait outside.

"No," she replied, without taking her eyes off her husband. Dr. Clark turned back to the table.

Dr. Perry made an incision in the President's throat and slipped a tube down the hole, performing a tracheotomy, giving John F. Kennedy one last chance to breathe.

Later, doctors described the procedures they performed to try to bring the President back to life. They hand pumped type O-negative blood into his left arm and leg. They pushed another tube into his chest to keep his lung from collapsing. They attached a machine to him to measure his heartbeat.

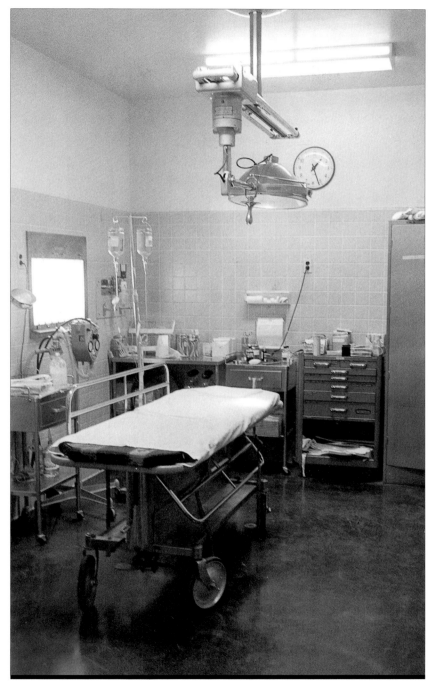

Emergency Room One

The needle on the machine showed only a straight line.

It was clearly hopeless. In fact, if it had been anyone but the President of the United States, he would have been declared D.O.A. at the hospital. But the doctors still worked.

Dr. Clark watched the straight line on the machine for a few moments, then leaned across the President's body and whispered to Dr. Perry. "It's too late, Mac," Dr. Clark said.

But Dr. Perry kept working. He kneeled on a stool over Jack Kennedy's body and kneaded his fist back and forth over the President's chest, as though he were trying to pump the heart himself. The machine still showed a straight line.

Dr. Perry was oblivious to everything around him except the man on the table and his own futile efforts to make the man's heart beat again. Three minutes passed. Dr. Perry kept trying to jolt his patient back to life. Five minutes. The machine still showed nothing but a straight line. Seven minutes. No one in the emergency room moved. Dr. Malcolm Perry kept working, trying to will Jack Kennedy's heart to beat. Ten minutes.

At last, Dr. Perry stepped back from the table. A doctor turned off the oxygen. Another doctor drew a clean sheet over the President's body. The Reverend Oscar Huber, a priest who had heard the news of the shooting on the radio and had raced to the hospital in case he was needed, entered the room and began administering the last rites of the Roman Catholic Church.

Jacqueline Kennedy stepped forward. She bent and kissed

her husband's foot, then took his right hand in her own. The priest intoned the familiar words, "Eternal rest, grant him, O Lord."

And Jacqueline Kennedy responded, "And let perpetual light shine on him."

Mrs. Kennedy then took a ring from her finger and placed it on one of her husband's. One by one, the people in the room slowly left.

Jacqueline Kennedy being escorted into a hearse waiting outside Parkland Hospital

EMERGENCY CASES ONLY

AMBULANCES ONLY

An anxious crowd gathering outside the emergency entrance of Parkland Hospital

While all of this was taking place in the emergency room, most reporters were trying to find a telephone to call in what little information was available. White House reporters who had gained entrance to the emergency area had heard the priest and also had talked with Secret Service agents, who described the President's wounds as "very bad." They were now prepared for the worst and were just waiting for an official announcement.

Upstairs in the hospital, however, we did not know what was happening on the floor below. After securing the phone in the lobby with Don, I headed off down one corridor of the hospital, looking for a way to the emergency area. Through the windows in offices I could see reporters trying to talk nurses and administrators into letting them use their telephones. I jostled my way past doctors, nurses, patients, and visitors.

Everyone in the hospital seemed to know the President had been shot and was in the emergency room downstairs and they were out in the corridors talking about it. I asked one man in a white coat the way to the emergency area and he pointed me toward a staircase. Before I found it, however, I overheard a man in a business suit telling some reporters that there would be a statement shortly in a nurses' classroom just across the hall. I decided I should get the statement and find Smitty later.

There were two doors leading into the room, one on either side of a small dais. A green blackboard was on the wall behind.

The first person I saw was Preston McGraw, sitting in one of those old-fashioned school desks with a writing arm.

"Hello, pardner," Mac said. "They're going to have a statement here in a minute."

"I've got a phone tied up in the lobby," I said.

"Have you seen Smitty?" Mac asked.

"No," I replied. "But I don't know what he looks like."

"There he is now," Mac said, maneuvering himself out of the school desk and nodding toward the door as some reporters came in. Mac greeted Smitty. They obviously knew each other.

A couple of television cameramen came in and began to set up their cameras on tripods a few feet away to film the news conference for broadcast later, which was the way television still had to cover most news events in those days.

Smitty looked like a reporter straight out of central casting. He wore a slightly rumpled suit, walked with a slouch, and actually talked out of the side of his mouth.

"Hi, Mac," Smitty said. "Still nothing official. This will be it."

At that moment one of the television cameramen bumped Smitty from behind. Smitty turned and grabbed the cameraman by the lapels and shoved him backward.

"Move it somewhere else," Smitty said. "We've got to get this."

It was all the cameraman could do to keep from falling over. He didn't say a word, but he moved the camera back.

Malcolm Kilduff

Just then two men in suits came in the room followed by a man in a white coat. All three stepped up on the dais and one of the men in a suit introduced the other two. One was a doctor and the other the hospital's administrator. I started to write their names, but I never finished. The man who was speaking was Malcolm Kilduff, the acting White House press secretary. The next thing he said was what we had all come to find out.

"President John Fitzgerald Kennedy died at approximately one o'clock."

I did not have to ask or be told what to do. No sooner were the words out of his mouth than I tore out of the room and

Reporters being briefed on the extent of President Kennedy's injuries

down the corridor toward the lobby. I can remember almost every step of that dash toward the phone. The hallway was crowded with people—nurses and interns, secretaries, patients, visitors.

The way I dodged through the crowd served as an alarm in itself. I might as well have been clanging a bell as I ran. People stopped and turned to look at me as though my race toward the phone was a confirmation of their worst fears.

I was followed out of the nurses' classroom by other reporters, all of whom were looking for a free telephone. I, on the other hand, had a phone waiting for me.

When I got to the lobby, I sprinted across it. A man was inside the phone booth, staring at the instrument, a coin in his hand. I don't know whether he had already tried to make a call, but he was clearly puzzled that the phone didn't work. I reached in front of him and grabbed the receiver.

"This phone is tied up," I said. The man silently backed out of the booth and stood a few feet away, staring at me.

"Don!" I shouted into the receiver, hoping nothing had gone wrong, that he was still on the other end of the line.

"What is it, Bill?"

"He's dead. It's official. He died at 1 P.M."

"Who said it?"

"The White House guy. Kilduff. Some hospital administrator was with him. I didn't get his name."

Suddenly it hit me, and my next words were almost a wail. I fought back tears as I repeated the news.

"My God, Don, he's dead. He's really dead."

Don shouted over to Jack. "It's official. Kilduff just announced it. He died at 1 P.M."

There was only a moment's pause and then through the phone line I could hear Jack all the way across the U.P.I. newsroom, all the way across town, as for the second time that day he uttered that command followed by words that would in seconds be typed out all across the country and around the world.

"FLASH!" Jack said, as though pronouncing a death sentence.

```
FLASH
PRESIDENT KENNEDY DEAD
```

Assuming the duties of President, Lyndon B. Johnson proclaimed a national day of mourning.

Chapter 7

Wwhat else have you got?" Don asked.

"That's it. I left as soon as he announced it. Mac's still at the news conference."

"Start a relay. We want every word."

I ran back to the nurses' classroom. Mac was standing near the door writing feverishly in his notebook. He glanced up at me. One of the doctors was speaking at the dais, explaining the procedures the medical staff had taken to try to save the President's life. As soon as I started writing, Mac moved to relay in what he had taken down.

"I'll call this in," Mac said. "Where's the phone?"

"The far side of the lobby."

He left. The doctor was speaking again and I wrote as fast as I've ever written, spelling words phonetically that I didn't even know the meaning of. As soon as Mac returned, I left to dictate what I had. It was on about my third trip back to the phone that Don had another task for me.

"Find out where Johnson is," Don said.

It was curious that until that point, I had not even thought about the Vice President. In fact, his name had not been mentioned in all the rush to get out the news about Kennedy. No one had seen Lyndon Johnson since shortly after he arrived at the hospital with the motorcade. And that contributed to the misunderstanding that followed, with embarrassing results for the Associated Press.

"He must be here at the hospital somewhere," I said.

"Try to find out exactly where Johnson is," Don said, a tenseness in his voice.

What Don didn't tell me and what I didn't learn until later was the reason behind the urgency of those orders. The A.P. had put out a Bulletin saying that Lyndon Johnson had suffered a heart attack. Someone had seen him holding his chest when he arrived at the hospital and that spawned a rumor about the heart attack that the A.P. had reported. It was not corrected for nearly an hour, and it was printed in some afternoon newspapers.

I had no idea how I was going to find out the whereabouts of Lyndon Johnson. But as it turned out, I didn't have much reporting to do. Just as I got back to the news conference to tell Mac my assignment, Smitty came over and told Mac that Kilduff advised the White House reporters to be prepared to leave soon. Johnson had already left for the airport and he would be sworn in as President by a federal judge aboard *Air Force One*, the Presidential jet, and the plane would then leave immediately for Washington. Mac turned to me.

"Phone that in," he said.

President Kennedy's coffin being loaded onto Air Force One

I ran back to the phone and told Don about the inauguration plans. That seemed to satisfy the office about Johnson's well-being. It was unlikely they were going to let the Vice President take the oath of office if he had just suffered a heart attack.

It was later that I learned what had happened to Johnson. Almost as soon as he arrived at the hospital, the Vice President was taken by Secret Service agents to a small waiting room in the emergency section of the hospital. No one at that point had any idea who was behind the attempt on the President's life. For all anyone knew, it could be part of a larger plot to take over the United States. And the most important person in the country at that moment was Lyndon B. Johnson.

Johnson was ushered into the little room, guarded by Secret Service agents with submachine guns. Nearby was the air force colonel carrying the small attaché case that always traveled with the President of the United States, the black case that contained all the codes for launching nuclear missiles and ordering the American bomber fleet to attack.

Johnson sat on an ambulance cart, his wife Lady Bird standing by him, and stared at the floor. He did not know what was happening across the hall in Emergency Room One until Ken O'Donnell, one of Kennedy's aides, came in to tell him the news. O'Donnell said later that he didn't know how to address Johnson. He couldn't just call him Lyndon. O'Donnell walked up to him and said, "Mr. President . . ."

Johnson's head shot up with a jolt and Lady Bird let out a gasp and put her hand to her mouth. It was the first either knew that Kennedy was dead.

Johnson left a short time later for the airport. But once he was there, he refused to board *Air Force One* until the Kennedy staff approved it. Then, once he was on, he refused to leave Dallas without the slain President's body and Mrs. Kennedy. There was also a delay in finding Judge Hughes and her arrival at the airport.

It was 2:38 P.M., central standard time, when Lyndon Baines Johnson stood in the packed cabin of *Air Force One*, his left hand on a small black Bible held by U.S. District Judge Sarah T. Hughes. He raised his right hand and before an audience of Kennedy White House staff, Secret Service agents, and reporters swore to faithfully execute the office of President of the United States and to preserve, protect, and defend the Constitution of the United States.

Vice President Johnson is sworn in as 36th President of the United States aboard Air Force One, flanked by his wife, Lady Bird, left, and Jacqueline Kennedy, right.

November 23 headlines bannering Kennedy's assassination

Once the White House press corps left for Love Field, the tension in the nurses' classroom at Parkland Hospital deflated like a punctured balloon. Mac and I sat at the little school desks and waited for the next developments. Someone brought in a coffee urn, a couple quarts of milk, a box of sugar, and some styrofoam cups. The telephone company arrived an hour or so later with about twenty pay phones, which they installed in what now had become a makeshift pressroom.

The doctors had not stayed long at the news conference after the White House officials and reporters departed and the local journalists took over what was left of the story in Dallas. The remainder of the story at Parkland was the condition of Governor Connally, who was going to recover. But it was minor news compared to what else had happened that day.

For the rest of the afternoon, the remaining reporters settled in to drinking stale coffee and waiting. At one point, some doctors came in and stepped up on the dais. They were going to hold a news conference about Governor Connally. I rushed to the front of the room and got my notebook out, ready to take down every word, set up another phone relay.

Mac came up beside me and put a hand on my arm.

"I don't think we'll have to take down every word on this one, pardner," he said. "Connally's just a sidebar. But we can both take notes to backstop each other."

About halfway through the news conference, Mac whispered to me, "I think I've got enough. I'll phone this in. You stay here in case they say anything."

As five o'clock approached, I began to have another fear. I was due to get off work at 5 P.M., and I was afraid that Jack would tell me to go home like he had done the previous day. I hated to even bring the subject up, hoping maybe they would just forget I was supposed to get off work then.

"Mac, there's something I need to ask you," I finally said.

"Sure, what is it?"

"Well, I came in to work at eight this morning," I began nervously. "I'm due off at five and I was wondering whether I should go home when I'm supposed to."

Mac gave me a curious look.

"Do you want to go home at five o'clock?"

"No! Not at all. But I asked Jack yesterday if he wanted me to stay late and help out and he told me to go home."

"I wouldn't worry about it, pardner," Mac said, a trace of a smile on his face. "I don't think Jack'll mind if you stay on overtime tonight."

We continued to check with the office every fifteen minutes or so and it was just after five o'clock when Mac came back from a trip to the phone and told me Jack wanted to talk to me. I hurried down the corridor, afraid he was now going to tell me I should leave.

"It seems to be pretty well wrapped up at the hospital," Jack began.

"They're going to have another medical bulletin on Connally in a few minutes," I interjected, trying to make it sound important so that he wouldn't order me home for the day.

"Mac can handle that," Jack said. "I want you to get down to the police headquarters. They've arrested a suspect."

I don't know why Jack sent me to police headquarters instead of Mac. But I didn't ask him. I was still on the story.

Officers standing guard at Dallas's homicide headquarters

Maneuvering through a crowd of reporters, a Dallas police detective holds aloft the rifle used to assassinate President Kennedy.

Chapter 9

It is odd that throughout that whole afternoon, before Jack said a suspect had been arrested, I had not thought of someone actually carrying out the assassination. In the pressure of covering the breaking news at the hospital, there had not been time to think much beyond the next minute. It was obvious, of course, that someone was responsible for shooting the President. But in my mind it was impersonal. "They" had killed Kennedy. With Jack's news about the arrest, the vague "they," on whom our subconscious blames so much, became more focused. A real person had taken a rifle, aimed it, pulled the trigger, and ended the life of the President of the United States.

On my way out of the hospital, my first thought was for my car. It hadn't crossed my mind since I abandoned it on Harry Hines Boulevard several hours earlier. What if it had been towed away by the police? Or stolen? It was not material concern for the car that prompted my anxiety. But it occurred to me that if the car was not there, I did not know how I would get to the Dallas police headquarters.

As I jogged across the huge front lawn of the hospital in the general direction of the freeway the full enormity of what had happened that day hit me like a bolt of lightning.

President Kennedy was dead.

I stopped by a giant live oak tree on that vast front lawn of Parkland Hospital and cried. I leaned against it and sobbed, all the anger and grief I had suppressed during the afternoon pouring out as I muttered to myself, "He's dead, he's really dead." I wept for perhaps a minute, maybe two, wiped my eyes on my sleeve, and ran on toward my car, which was still there, and drove off to cover the rest of the story.

As I arrived at the Dallas police headquarters, I took my press card out of my wallet and put it in my pocket, ready to show it to whomever might challenge me. But no one ever asked to see it, an early indication of the loose security at the Dallas police headquarters that would have disastrous results later.

I made my way up to the third floor, to the homicide division. There were signs saying which way to go, but I didn't need them. All I had to do was follow the noise.

If the scene at Parkland Hospital had been chaotic, the one at the Dallas police headquarters was pandemonium. The corridor outside the office of Captain Will Fritz, the chief of homicide, was jammed. Reporters stood elbow to elbow, virtually unable to move. It was as though someone had ordered a fire drill and told everybody in the building to report to that one spot.

Captain Will Fritz

Television cables ran the length of the hallway and each crew had its lights turned on, bathing the corridor outside the homicide office in brilliant white light, like a movie set waiting for the big scene to unfold. In the days before satellites and modern video technology allowed live coverage of just about anything, television cameramen mostly had to film reports of such events for showing on the air later.

The prime suspect facing the press at the Dallas police station

Every scrap of information about the shooting and the man the police believed did it was instantly relayed around the world by wire in a running story to newspapers that were printing special editions and to television stations that were preempting all programming for nonstop coverage. There was no other news story in the world that day.

I inched my way through the crowd and finally saw Terry McGarry, another U.P.I. reporter, in a detective squad room across the hall from Captain Fritz's office. Terry was sitting at a desk talking on the telephone. He motioned me over.

"They just charged Oswald with killing the cop," Terry said after he had hung up the phone.

"What cop?" I asked. "And who's Oswald?"

"You'd better let me fill you in."

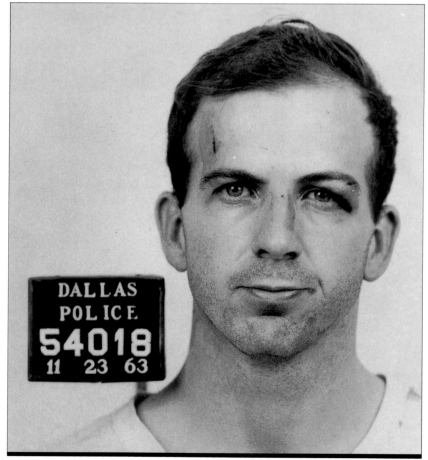

Lee Harvey Oswald

The man the police had in custody had been arrested in the Oak Cliff section of Dallas, just across the Trinity River from the downtown area. A Dallas policeman named J.D. Tippit had been gunned down on a street in Oak Cliff a short time after the President had been shot. Witnesses had seen a man with a gun run into the Texas Theater, a movie house on Jefferson Avenue, and the police went in after him. When they turned the lights on in the theater, the man jumped up and tried to shoot one of the policemen. The gun misfired and the police arrested him.

The man's name was Lee Harvey Oswald. The police said that in addition to being accused of shooting Patrolman Tippit, he was also a suspect in the killing of President Kennedy.

Oswald was an employee at the Texas School Book Depository, a textbook warehouse located on Elm Street just at the spot where the President was shot. In the moments after the shooting, Secret Service agents and the Dallas police swarmed over the building, searching it. On the sixth floor, they found a rifle with a telescopic sight and some chicken bones. Oswald's supervisor noticed that he was missing. He told the police that one of his employees had left work.

The police immediately put out an all points bulletin that the employee, Lee Harvey Oswald, was to be picked up for questioning. His description followed: white male, about five feet six inches, 150 pounds, twenty-four years of age, dark hair, wearing a dark jacket.

The shots were fired from the sixth-floor corner window, shown by arrow, of the Texas School Book Depository.

According to evidence released later, as well as some reporting I did afterward, Oswald's movements on the day of the
assassination became clear. Oswald carried the rifle he used in
the assassination to work with him that day wrapped up in
paper. He had retrieved it that morning from its hiding place
in the garage of Mrs. Ruth Paine, a woman with whom his wife,
Marina, lived in Irving, a suburb of Dallas. Oswald himself
lived at a rooming house in Oak Cliff, but he often visited his

wife at Mrs. Paine's on weekends. Oswald had surprised them the night before by showing up in Irving on a weeknight. A neighbor who drove Oswald back into Dallas the next morning asked him what he had rolled up in the paper. "Curtain rods," Oswald had replied.

As the time for the President's motorcade approached, many employees at the School Book Depository went outside on their lunch break on that warm November day to try to catch a glimpse of Kennedy as he passed. Oswald, on the other hand, took some fried chicken up to the sixth floor of the building, moved some book cartons to make himself a sniper's post, and quietly ate his lunch, waiting for the President's limousine to move into the crosshairs on the telescopic sight of his rifle.

The sniper's post

After firing the shots, Oswald walked out of the building and caught a bus headed for Oak Cliff. Such was the state of Lee Harvey Oswald's mind that he apparently thought he could escape from assassinating the President of the United States on a city bus.

When the bus became stuck in traffic, Oswald got off. He walked over to the Greyhound bus terminal on Commerce Street and got into a taxi. He directed the cab to Oak Cliff and got out at a corner about two blocks beyond his rooming house on Beckley Street and walked back. Oswald's room was in the main part of the house and as he walked in the front door, the housekeeper was watching news of the assassination on television. Without saying a word to her, Oswald went into his room. He changed his jacket, from a dark one to a light one, put a .38-caliber pistol in his pocket, and went back out.

Patrolman J.D. Tippit

Dallas patrolman J.D. Tippit was driving down 10th Street when he saw a man walking along who fit the description of the A.P.B. that had been broadcast on the police radio. Only the jacket was different. He stopped his patrol car and got out to ask the man some questions. As he approached, Oswald pulled out his .38 and fired four bullets into Patrolman Tippit and continued walking down the street.

The first time I saw Lee Harvey Oswald was on one of the many trips he made between his jail cell on the fifth floor of the Dallas police headquarters and the homicide office on the third floor. They brought him down several times that night to be questioned. The detectives would interrogate him for about half an hour, then take him back to his cell upstairs.

On every trip Oswald made to be questioned, I elbowed my way to the front of the pack of reporters and photographers who had jammed the corridor that led from the elevators to Captain Fritz's office. As he walked those few yards, surrounded by police detectives and bathed in the TV lights, he was bombarded by questions from journalists while flashbulbs popped. I jostled and edged my way along with him every step of the way.

Oswald being brought from his cell to the homicide bureau for questioning

He was handcuffed and he had a small cut on his forehead above his right eye, the result, I learned later, of the fight with the policemen who arrested him in the theater. His left eye was also slightly swollen and bruised. He kept a sort of grim smile on his face. It occurred to me that he was enjoying all the attention, being in the spotlight.

A handcuffed Oswald being led through the Dallas police station

I never asked any questions on those trips down the corridor, but I wrote down every word he said and gesture he made. As soon as he would disappear into the homicide office, I would claw my way out of the pack and find the first phone and call in what he had said. Jack was writing a running story and each detail I phoned in was going straight onto the wire.

Most of the questions were variations on the same theme, the one thing everyone wanted to know, the one question to which there seemed no answer: Why?

"Why did you do it, Lee?" most would ask, immediately assuming a first-name basis with him, as reporters often do, whether they are talking to a movie star, a politician, or a killer. Occasionally someone would ask, "How did you get hurt, Lee?" or "Why did you shoot Connally, Lee?" Actually, I thought I knew the answer to that last one. It was because he was there.

Oswald never answered any of the questions directly. But he would sometimes lean over to speak into one of the outstretched microphones. He mostly muttered slogans.

"Call the A.C.L.U.," he appealed to the crowd of reporters on one trip, referring to the American Civil Liberties Union, an organization known for defending civil rights. "I demand my hygienic rights," Oswald said on another trip. No one quite knew what he meant by that.

Throughout the night, Oswald denied it all. "I didn't shoot anybody," he said over and over.

Most of the reporters at the police headquarters seemed to

think the police had gotten their man. He was the chief suspect, and if there were any doubts about his innocence they were not expressed that night.

Every hour brought more reporters from around the world. A crew from French television had chartered a plane and arrived about 9 P.M. There were already reporters from London papers and the British Broadcasting Corporation. The switchboard at the Dallas police headquarters was jammed with calls from all over the world, asking questions and offering suggestions to the police.

From the beginning, possibly out of a civic sense of guilt or responsibility, the Dallas police seemed to bend over backward to accommodate the reporters descending on the city. The detectives' offices and the squad rooms were thrown open to reporters, who would often grab the first telephone they saw on any desk and place calls to far-flung points around the globe.

Between Oswald's trips, I tried to strike up conversations with the police detectives working the case to find out any tidbit of information I could.

One of the detectives I got to know told me that a man called from Australia to suggest the police pump Oswald's stomach. If there were any traces of chicken in his digestive system, the Australian explained, it would prove he was guilty. Another man called from Germany and advised the police not to let Oswald wash his hands until they had run a paraffin test on him to see if he had fired a gun. "Who do they think we are here?" the detective asked. "It was the first thing we did."

At one point in the evening, the police brought in Oswald's mother and his wife. Later a Dallas police detective brought in the rifle, holding it aloft like a trophy while photographers' flashbulbs popped.

Marina Oswald

It was shortly before midnight when Captain Fritz finally said the case was "cinched" and the police charged him with the President's murder. An affidavit on behalf of the State of Texas stated that Lee Harvey Oswald did "voluntarily and with malice aforethought kill John F. Kennedy by shooting him with a gun."

6.5 ITALIAN CARBINE
Late military issue. Only 40" over-
all. Weighs 7 lbs. Shows only slight
use, test-fired and head spaced, ready
for shooting. Turned-down bolt, 6-
shot, clip fed, rear sight,
thumb safety.   **$12⁷⁸**
C20-1196 . . . .
C20-750. Carbine with brand new 4X
scope—¾" dia. (illustrated) **$19.95**
E20-751. 6.5mm Italian military am-
mo, 108 rds. (6-shot clip free) **$7.50**

An ad from Klein's Sporting Goods, the Chicago mail-order house
from which Oswald ordered his weapon

The body of the President lies in state at the Capitol rotunda.

Chapter 10

The rest of the weekend was almost anticlimactic for me. I got home from the police headquarters about 2 A.M. with orders to be back at work the following morning at eight. I no longer felt like a fifth wheel in the office.

The focus of the story returned to Washington, where Kennedy's body was lying in state in the Capitol rotunda and dignitaries from around the world were flying in for the funeral.

Members of the Kennedy family listening to a eulogy for the slain President

But there was still plenty of reporting to do in Dallas as the investigation into the President's murder continued. As more information about Oswald emerged, I was one of the reporters sent off to chase down any details we could find about him. I interviewed Mrs. Paine in Irving and his landlady in Oak Cliff. Every chance I had, I looked in on the television coverage of the solemn events being played out in Washington. The whole world seemed to be in mourning.

An unknown sailor mourning the loss of the President

On Sunday, I was given the morning off. It seemed like I had eaten nothing and had slept only a few hours in the previous two days. I had subsisted mostly on coffee and excitement.

The Dallas police had announced that they planned to transfer Oswald from his cell in police headquarters to the more secure county jail at the other end of town on Sunday morning at 11 A.M. No one in the press believed them.

The thinking among reporters was that announcing the time for the transfer was only a ruse and the police would likely move Oswald in the middle of the night. Jack decided to keep a reporter on the scene all night and he sent me over to the headquarters about 10 P.M. By this time I had learned that one of the features of journalism, even on big stories, is waiting. Like movie stars, reporters have brief periods of intense activity followed by hours of waiting for the next thing to happen. So I settled in at police headquarters to wait.

For the next few hours, I drank a lot of coffee, tried to talk to some detectives, who had by now become notably less talkative, and phoned the office every twenty minutes or so. At about 3 A.M., another reporter relieved me and I was told to go home and get some sleep and report to the county jail at noon, by which time Oswald should have been transferred.

I went to church with my parents the next morning, planning to leave services early so I could get to the county jail by noon. When I got to my car, I turned on the radio and heard the news that Oswald had just been shot as the police escorted him into an underground parking garage.

Detectives lead Oswald to an underground garage.

Jack Ruby steps from a crowd of reporters and pulls a gun.

While millions of Americans watch on live television, Jack Ruby shoots Lee Harvey Oswald.

My first reaction was of disbelief. I could not understand how such a thing could happen while Oswald was in police custody. If there was a fleeting sense that some sort of Wild West justice had been carried out, it disappeared as I realized in a moment that if Oswald died, the answers to a thousand questions about the assassination of Kennedy would die with him.

I found the first phone I could and called U.P.I. Jack told me Oswald was listed in serious condition and had been taken to Parkland Hospital. I thought I might go back there, but other reporters were already there and Jack said that I should come into the office.

Most of America had seen the shooting of the man charged with killing Kennedy live on television. The networks had wanted to set up cameras and bring in their mobile units to televise the transfer of the prisoner live. And the Dallas police, in their desire to please the world's press, had stuck to their schedule.

As a result, security at Dallas police headquarters had been lax. And along with all the reporters and photographers and television crews who entered the underground parking garage that morning to record Oswald's transfer was another man. His name was Jack Ruby. He operated some nightclubs in Dallas and he was a familiar face to many Dallas policemen.

When the police brought Oswald down to the parking garage where an armored car was waiting to take him to the county jail, Ruby pulled a pistol, stepped forward, and with the world watching, shot him at point-blank range. Oswald

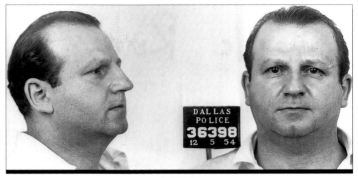

Jack Ruby

Ruby being led through the Dallas city jail in handcuffs

died two hours later at Parkland Hospital, in the same room his victim had.

Within an hour of the death of the only suspect the police had, Captain Fritz announced that the case of the State of Texas vs. Lee Harvey Oswald in the murder of John F. Kennedy was "closed."

Police and detectives escorting the body of Lee Harvey Oswald from Parkland Hospital

Jacqueline Kennedy holds the hands of her children, Caroline and John Jr., following a memorial service honoring her slain husband. Behind her are, left to right, Attorney General Robert F. Kennedy, Jean Kennedy Smith, Patricia Kennedy Lawford, and Steven Smith.

Epilogue

The following day the horrible events in Dallas and the twisted life and violent death of Lee Harvey Oswald were briefly forgotten while the nation, through television, attended the funeral of its fallen leader.

No one who saw it can ever forget the dignity with which Jackie Kennedy led the nation in its mourning. The images from those days burned into one's memory. There was the heart-rending sight of John F. Kennedy Jr., or John-John as he was known then at the age of three, saluting his father's casket. There was the long cortege of limousines following the flag-draped coffin as it was slowly pulled on a horse-drawn caisson, a riderless black stallion named Black Jack prancing behind, while martial bands played the tunes of glory. And there was the veiled Mrs. Kennedy walking solemnly at the head of an assemblage of kings, presidents, and prime ministers who had traveled from around the world to pay their last respects.

The assassination of President Kennedy is regarded by many as a turning point in the nation's history, an event that has become a benchmark in the lives of all who remember it.

The horse-drawn caisson en route from St. Matthew's Cathedral to Arlington National Cemetery

John Kennedy Jr.
saluting the casket
of his slain father

Jacqueline Kennedy

Black Jack,
the riderless horse,
following the casket

Robert Kennedy being comforted by two of his children on the lawn of his Virginia home

It certainly changed the direction of my life. Being involved in the coverage of those events was like being in the eye of a tornado with the terrible winds of history swirling around me, fearful yet exhilarating.

At the time I went to work for U.P.I., I still was not sure what I wanted to do in life. But the excitement of that day left me determined to pursue a career in journalism. Just over two years later, Jack Fallon was promoted to foreign editor of U.P.I. and returned to New York. He arranged for my transfer there, too, and after two years of working on the foreign cables desk in New York, I was assigned to London as a foreign correspondent.

Bill Hampton in 1996

Since then I have covered many big stories, from wars and riots to summit meetings and world conferences, from hijackings and coups to international sporting championships and even other assassinations.

But it soon became clear to me that no matter how many front-page stories I covered or how many Bulletins I wrote, I had covered the biggest story of my life on November 22, 1963, and that nothing I did later would ever be quite the same.

"If we cannot end now our differences, at least we can help make the world safe for diversity. For, in the final analysis, our most basic common link is that we all inhabit this small planet. We all breathe the same air. We all cherish our children's future. And we all are mortal."

John Fitzgerald Kennedy
1917–1963

Commencement Address
American University, June 11, 1963

This book would not exist without the help of many people. First of all, it would never have been written had not Mary Pope Osborne suggested it and urged me to undertake it. The enthusiasm of Amy Ehrlich encouraged me to continue and provided a source of strength. Susan Halperin was immensely helpful in editing the book and Ann Stott brought it into focus with her designing eye. Bruce Frost gave early guidance and support and Kate Schwartz and Valerie Dumova provided the final polish. It would be remiss of me not to acknowledge the legion of reporters and photographers who covered the assassination more ably than I. Finally, as with everything good in my life, it is a reflection of the abiding inspiration of my wife, LuAnn Walther.

American Heritage Publishing Co., Inc., and United Press International, comps. *Four Days: The Historical Record of the Death of President Kennedy.* American Heritage Publishing Co., Inc., 1964.

Associated Press. *The Torch Is Passed.* Western Printing and Lithographing Co., 1964.

Bishop, Jim. *The Day Kennedy Was Shot.* New York: Funk & Wagnalls, 1968.

The Dallas Morning News. *November 22: The Day Remembered.* Dallas: Taylor Publishing Company, 1990.

PHOTO CREDITS

Newspaper articles on jacket and endpapers:
U.P.I. news articles reprinted courtesy of United Press International.
Article on the death of John F. Kennedy by Jean Dietz reprinted courtesy of the *Boston Globe*.
Article about the Kennedy assassination taken from a MARY McGRORY column by Mary McGrory.
  Dist. by UNIVERSAL PRESS SYNDICATE. Reprinted with permission. All rights reserved.